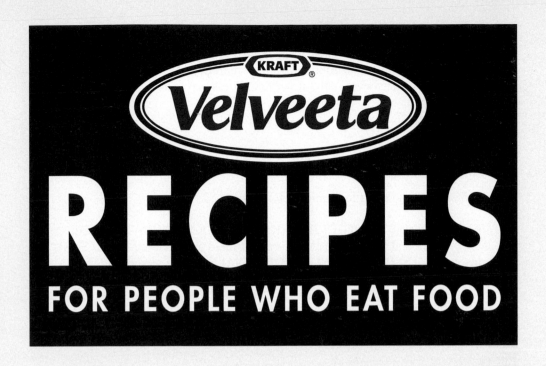

KRAFT®
Velveeta
RECIPES
FOR PEOPLE WHO EAT FOOD

D0579175

Publications International, Ltd.

Favorite Brand Name Recipes at www.fbnr.com

VELVEETA, VELVEETA LIGHT, BREAKSTONE'S, KNUDSEN, MINUTE, MIRACLE WHIP and OSCAR MAYER are registered trademarks of Kraft Foods Holdings, Inc. TACO BELL and HOME ORIGINALS are registered trademarks owned and licensed by Taco Bell Corp.

Kraft Kitchens Division Manager: Denise Henderson
Kraft Kitchens Consumer Foods Manager: Lori Bowen Tillock
Kraft Kitchens Technician: Cathy Zenner
Recipe Testing: Lori Hartnett
Associate Brand Manager: John Gray
Assistant Brand Manager: Karen Droegemueller
Consumer Promotions Assistant: Lisa Smith

Photography: Stephen Hamilton Photographics, Inc.
Photographers: Stephen Hamilton, Jennifer Marks
Photographers' Assistants: Lia Dickinson, Tate Hunt
Prop Stylist: Paula Walters
Prop Stylist's Assistant: Tom Hamilton
Food Stylists: Carol Parik, Judy Vance
Assistant Food Stylist: Susie Skoog

Pictured on the front cover: Salsa Dip *(page 8)*.

Pictured on the back cover *(top to bottom)*: 15 Minute Cheesy Chicken and Vegetable Rice *(page 50)*, Twice Baked Ranch Potatoes *(page 54)* and Cheeseburger Mac *(page 30)*.

ISBN: 0-7853-5175-2

Manufactured in U.S.A.

8 7 6 5 4 3 2 1

Microwave Cooking: Microwave ovens vary in wattage. Use the cooking times as guidelines and check for doneness before adding more time.

Preparation/Cooking Times: Preparation times are based on the approximate amount of time required to assemble the recipe before cooking, baking, chilling or serving. These times include preparation steps such as measuring, chopping and mixing. The fact that some preparations and cooking can be done simultaneously is taken into account. Preparation of optional ingredients and serving suggestions is not included.

WELCOME TO THE WONDERFUL WORLD OF VELVEETA

What fun you can have with versatile VELVEETA®! It's "JUST THE THING" you need more often than any other food in your refrigerator. It spreads, slices, toasts or melts to perfection every time. Just the thing for spur of the moment parties, because with VELVEETA you can turn out swell toasted sandwiches or make a delightful cheese dip in no time flat. It's a great helper with main dishes too! VELVEETA is on your side; it is your best friend. It makes your life easy, because it is user friendly—easy to operate—and this book is its manual. FOR A CLEAN PLATE EVERY TIME!™, keep the 2-pound loaf of versatile VELVEETA ever ready. It pays to get Kraft's famous prepared cheese product, genuine VELVEETA.

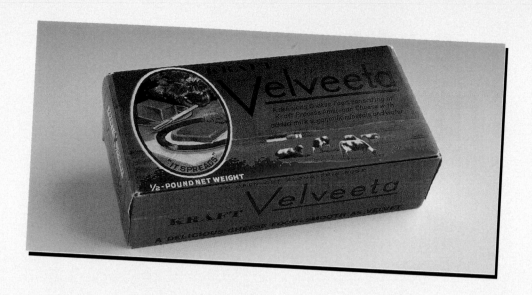

Just as America has grown up with VELVEETA, so has VELVEETA grown up with America. VELVEETA has been melting into moms' most warmly anticipated recipes since 1928. Using breakthrough technology, Kraft introduced VELVEETA to North America as the first ever pasteurized, process cheese food. VELVEETA quickly became and has remained the leading process cheese for nearly 70 years. With its creamy melting characteristics and deliciously mild flavor, VELVEETA appeals to everyone in your family from young children to adults. The familiar yellow box is an American icon with timeless appeal— a reminder that we're dedicated to providing you with what you like, what you want and what you've come to trust from Kraft.

DIPS THAT GET DEVOURED

Baseball. The great American pastime. Each year we spend hours as spectators watching...absolutely nothing happens. As Americans we deserve a national pastime with more personal involvement. Like eating. It's something that we have been doing since we were born, so we're already good at it. Like the icon of the baseball, eating would also have an icon of its own: a large bowl of VELVEETA dip. Dips That Get Devoured represent all of the different dips that one can use to participate in this wonderfully rich activity.

Salsa Dip

Prep Time: 5 minutes   Microwave Time: 5 minutes

1 pound (16 ounces) VELVEETA Pasteurized Prepared Cheese Product, cut up

1 cup TACO BELL HOME ORIGINALS Thick 'N Chunky Salsa

1. Microwave VELVEETA and salsa in 1½-quart microwavable bowl on HIGH 5 minutes or until VELVEETA is melted, stirring after 3 minutes. Serve hot with tortilla chips or cut-up vegetables.   *Makes 3 cups*

Salsa Dip

Layered Mexican Dip

Prep Time: 5 minutes   Microwave Time: 6 minutes

1 can (16 ounces) refried beans

¾ pound (12 ounces) VELVEETA Pasteurized Prepared Cheese Product, cut up

½ cup TACO BELL HOME ORIGINALS Thick 'N Chunky Salsa

1. Spread beans on bottom of 9-inch microwavable pie plate or quiche dish. Top with VELVEETA and salsa.

2. Microwave on HIGH 5 to 6 minutes or until VELVEETA is melted, turning every 2 minutes. Serve hot with tortilla chips.

Makes about 2 cups

Onion Chip Dip

Prep Time: 5 minutes   Microwave Time: 5 minutes

1 pound (16 ounces) VELVEETA Pasteurized Prepared Cheese Product, cut up

1 container (8 ounces) BREAKSTONE'S or KNUDSEN Sour Cream

2 tablespoons chopped green onion

1. Microwave VELVEETA in 1½-quart microwavable bowl on HIGH 4 minutes or until melted, stirring after 2 minutes.

2. Stir in sour cream and onion. Microwave 1 minute. Serve hot with potato chips.

Makes 2¾ cups

Layered Mexican Dip

Cheeseburger Dip

Prep Time: 5 minutes   Cook Time: 10 minutes

½ pound ground beef

1 pound (16 ounces) VELVEETA Pasteurized Prepared Cheese Product, cut up

¼ cup milk <u>or</u> water

2 tablespoons <u>each</u> KRAFT Pure Prepared Mustard and catsup

1. Brown meat in skillet; drain. Reduce heat to low.

2. Add VELVEETA, milk, mustard and catsup; stir until VELVEETA is melted. Serve hot with French fries or tortilla chips.

Makes 2¾ cups

Fiesta Jalapeño & Tomato Dip

Prep Time: 10 minutes   Microwave Time: 5 minutes

1 pound (16 ounces) VELVEETA Mexican Pasteurized Process Cheese Spread with Jalapeño Peppers, cut up

½ cup chopped tomato

⅛ teaspoon garlic powder (optional)

1. Microwave VELVEETA, tomato and garlic powder in 2-quart microwavable bowl on HIGH 4 to 5 minutes or until VELVEETA is melted, stirring every 2 minutes. Serve hot with tortilla chips.

Makes 1¾ cups

Cheeseburger Dip

Vegetable Dip

Prep Time: 5 minutes   Microwave Time: 5 minutes

1 pound (16 ounces) VELVEETA Pasteurized Prepared Cheese
  Product, cut up

1 container (16 ounces) BREAKSTONE'S or KNUDSEN Sour Cream

1 package (0.9 ounces) vegetable soup mix

1. Microwave all ingredients in 2-quart microwavable bowl on HIGH
5 minutes or until VELVEETA is melted, stirring after 3 minutes. Serve
hot or cold with cut-up vegetables or crackers.   *Makes 3 cups*

Ranch Dip

Prep Time: 5 minutes   Microwave Time: 5 minutes

1 pound (16 ounces) VELVEETA Pasteurized Prepared Cheese
  Product, cut up

1 container (8 ounces) BREAKSTONE'S or KNUDSEN Sour Cream

1 cup KRAFT Ranch Dressing

1. Microwave VELVEETA in 1½-quart microwavable bowl on HIGH
4 minutes or until melted, stirring after 2 minutes.

2. Stir in sour cream and dressing. Microwave 1 minute. Serve hot
with potato chips or cut-up vegetables.   *Makes 3 cups*

*Top to bottom: Vegetable Dip
and Ranch Dip*

Bean Dip Olé

Prep Time: 5 minutes   Microwave Time: 9 minutes

1 pound (16 ounces) VELVEETA Pasteurized Prepared Cheese Product, cut up

1 can (16 ounces) refried beans

1 can (4 ounces) chopped green chilies

1. Microwave VELVEETA, beans and chilies in 2-quart microwavable bowl on HIGH 8 to 9 minutes or until VELVEETA is melted, stirring every 4 minutes. Serve hot with tortilla chips.   *Makes 3 cups*

Spinach Dip

Prep Time: 5 minutes   Microwave Time: 7 minutes

1 pound (16 ounces) VELVEETA LIGHT Pasteurized Prepared Cheese Product, cut up

1 can (14½ ounces) tomatoes, whole, cut up <u>or</u> diced, drained

1 package (10 ounces) frozen chopped spinach, thawed, drained

¼ teaspoon red pepper flakes

1. Microwave VELVEETA LIGHT and tomatoes in 1-quart microwavable bowl on HIGH 5 minutes or until VELVEETA LIGHT is completely melted, stirring after 2 minutes.

2. Stir in remaining ingredients. Microwave on HIGH 2 minutes or until thoroughly heated. Serve hot with bread sticks, tortilla chips or assorted cut-up vegetables.   *Makes 3 cups*

Sour Cream 'N Bacon Dip

Prep Time: 5 minutes   Microwave Time: 5 minutes

1 pound (16 ounces) VELVEETA Pasteurized Prepared Cheese Product, cut up

1 container (8 ounces) BREAKSTONE'S <u>or</u> KNUDSEN Sour Cream

2 tablespoons OSCAR MAYER Real Bacon Bits

1. Microwave VELVEETA in 1½-quart microwavable bowl on HIGH 4 minutes or until melted, stirring after 2 minutes.

2. Stir in sour cream and bacon bits. Microwave 1 minute. Serve hot with potato chips.   *Makes 2½ cups*

<u>*Make-Ahead Directions:*</u> *VELVEETA dips can travel to any party. Simply assemble ingredients at home in a zipper-style plastic bag and tote. At the party, transfer ingredients into microwavable bowl and heat according to recipe directions.*

Creamy Taco Dip

Prep Time: 5 minutes   Microwave Time: 5 minutes

- 1 pound (16 ounces) VELVEETA Pasteurized Prepared Cheese Product, cut up
- 1 container (16 ounces) BREAKSTONE'S or KNUDSEN Sour Cream
- 1 package (1¼ ounces) TACO BELL HOME ORIGINALS Taco Seasoning Mix

1. Microwave all ingredients in 2-quart microwavable bowl on HIGH 5 minutes or until VELVEETA is melted, stirring after 3 minutes. Serve hot or cold with corn chips or tortilla chips.   *Makes 3½ cups*

Mexican Dip

Prep Time: 5 minutes   Microwave Time: 5 minutes

- 1 pound (16 ounces) VELVEETA Mexican Pasteurized Process Cheese Spread with Jalapeño Peppers, cut up
- 1 container (8 ounces) BREAKSTONE'S or KNUDSEN Sour Cream

1. Microwave VELVEETA in 1½-quart microwavable bowl on HIGH 4 minutes or until melted, stirring after 2 minutes.

2. Stir in sour cream. Microwave 1 minute. Serve hot with tortilla chips or cut-up vegetables.   *Makes 2½ cups*

Creamy Taco Dip

Broccoli Dip

Prep Time: 5 minutes   Microwave Time: 6 minutes

1 package (10 ounces) frozen chopped broccoli

1 pound (16 ounces) VELVEETA Pasteurized Prepared Cheese
   Product, cut up

⅛ teaspoon garlic powder

1. Microwave broccoli in covered 2-quart microwavable bowl on
HIGH 3 minutes or until thawed; drain.

2. Add VELVEETA and garlic powder. Microwave 2 to 3 minutes or
until VELVEETA is melted, stirring after 2 minutes. Serve hot with
crackers and assorted cut-up vegetables.   *Makes 2¾ cups*

*Serving Suggestion: Try serving Broccoli Dip
in an edible bread bowl. Cut a lengthwise
slice from the top of a 1-pound round or oval
bread loaf. Remove bread from center,
leaving a 1-inch-thick bread shell. Pour in
your hot Broccoli Dip and serve.*

Broccoli Dip

Cheesy Chili Dip

Prep Time: 5 minutes   Microwave Time: 5 minutes

1 pound (16 ounces) VELVEETA Pasteurized Prepared Cheese Product, cut up

1 can (15 ounces) chili

1. Microwave VELVEETA and chili in 2-quart microwavable bowl on HIGH 5 minutes or until VELVEETA is melted, stirring after 3 minutes. Serve hot with tortilla chips, French bread chunks or corn bread sticks.

Makes 3¾ cups

Con Queso Dip

Prep Time: 5 minutes   Microwave Time: 5 minutes

1 pound (16 ounces) VELVEETA Pasteurized Prepared Cheese Product, cut up

1 can (10 ounces) diced tomatoes and green chilies, drained

1. Microwave VELVEETA and tomatoes and green chilies in 1½-quart microwavable bowl on HIGH 5 minutes or until VELVEETA is melted, stirring after 3 minutes. Serve hot with tortilla chips.

Makes 2¼ cups

*Top to bottom: Cheesy Chili Dip
and Con Queso Dip*

ONE PAN PLEASERS®

From the first tempting forkful to the last delicious morsel, your family will relish these One Pan Pleaser recipes. Each recipe requires only a few ingredients and is made quickly and easily in one pan. The rich mild cheddar taste of VELVEETA is the secret. You'll be pleased with the way VELVEETA cooks.... satin smooth and golden good.

Cheesy Beef Stroganoff

Prep Time: 10 minutes   Cook Time: 15 minutes

1 pound ground beef

2 cups water

3 cups (6 ounces) medium egg noodles, uncooked

¾ pound (12 ounces) VELVEETA Pasteurized Prepared Cheese Product, cut up

1 can (10¾ ounces) condensed cream of mushroom soup

¼ teaspoon black pepper

1. Brown meat in large skillet; drain.

2. Stir in water. Bring to boil. Stir in noodles. Reduce heat to medium-low; cover. Simmer 8 minutes or until noodles are tender.

3. Add VELVEETA, soup and pepper; stir until VELVEETA is melted.

Makes 4 to 6 servings

Cheesy Beef Stroganoff

Salsa Mac

Prep Time: 10 minutes   Cook Time: 15 minutes

1 pound ground beef

1 jar (16 ounces) TACO BELL HOME ORIGINALS
     Thick 'N Chunky Salsa

1¾ cups water

2 cups (8 ounces) elbow macaroni, uncooked

¾ pound (12 ounces) VELVEETA Pasteurized Prepared Cheese
     Product, cut up

1. Brown meat in large skillet; drain.

2. Stir in salsa and water. Bring to boil. Stir in macaroni. Reduce heat to medium-low; cover. Simmer 8 to 10 minutes or until macaroni is tender.

3. Add VELVEETA; stir until melted.   *Makes 4 to 6 servings*

Spicy Substitute: For an extra spicy kick in Salsa Mac, try making it with VELVEETA Mild or Hot Mexican Pasteurized Process Cheese Spread with Jalapeño Peppers. Be careful though . . . the hot is <u>really</u> hot!

Salsa Mac

Tuna & Noodles

Prep Time: 10 minutes   Cook Time: 15 minutes

2¼ cups water

3 cups (6 ounces) medium egg noodles, uncooked

¾ pound (12 ounces) VELVEETA Pasteurized Prepared Cheese Product, cut up

1 package (16 ounces) frozen vegetable blend, thawed, drained

1 can (6 ounces) tuna, drained, flaked

¼ teaspoon black pepper

1. Bring water to boil in saucepan. Stir in noodles. Reduce heat to medium-low; cover. Simmer 8 minutes or until noodles are tender.

2. Add VELVEETA, vegetables, tuna and pepper; stir until VELVEETA is melted.   *Makes 4 to 6 servings*

Take a Shortcut: When cooking pasta for Tuna & Noodles, you can double the amount you make and save half for a meal later in the week. Thoroughly drain the pasta you're not using, then put it in a bowl of ice water to stop the cooking. Drain thoroughly, then toss with 1 to 2 teaspoons of oil. Store in a zipper-style plastic bag in the refrigerator for up to 3 days.

Tuna & Noodles

Cheeseburger Mac

Prep Time: 10 minutes   Cook Time: 15 minutes

1 pound ground beef

2¾ cups water

⅓ cup catsup

1 to 2 teaspoons onion powder

2 cups (8 ounces) elbow macaroni, uncooked

¾ pound (12 ounces) VELVEETA Pasteurized Prepared Cheese Product, cut up

1. Brown meat in large skillet; drain.

2. Stir in water, catsup and onion powder. Bring to boil. Stir in macaroni. Reduce heat to medium-low; cover. Simmer 8 to 10 minutes or until macaroni is tender.

3. Add VELVEETA; stir until melted.   *Makes 4 to 6 servings*

<u>Safe Food Handling</u>: Store ground beef in the coldest part of the refrigerator for up to 2 days. Make sure raw juices do not touch other foods. Ground meat can be wrapped airtight and frozen for up to 3 months.

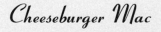

Cheesy Chicken & Broccoli Macaroni

Prep Time: 10 minutes   **Cook Time: 15 minutes**

4 boneless skinless chicken breast halves
(about 1¼ pounds), cut into chunks

1 can (14½ ounces) chicken broth

2 cups (8 ounces) elbow macaroni, uncooked

¾ pound (12 ounces) VELVEETA Pasteurized Prepared Cheese
Product, cut up

1 package (10 ounces) frozen chopped broccoli, thawed

1. Spray large skillet with no stick cooking spray. Add chicken; cook and stir on medium-high heat 2 minutes or until no longer pink.

2. Stir in broth. Bring to boil. Stir in macaroni. Reduce heat to medium-low; cover. Simmer 8 to 10 minutes or until macaroni is tender.

3. Add VELVEETA and broccoli; stir until VELVEETA is melted.

Makes 4 to 6 servings

<u>A Variation:</u> Cheesy Chicken & Broccoli Rice: Substitute 2 cups uncooked MINUTE Rice for macaroni. Cook chicken as directed. Add broth; bring to boil. Add rice, VELVEETA and broccoli; stir. Cover. Remove from heat. Let stand 10 minutes. Stir until melted.

Cheesy Chicken & Broccoli Macaroni

Tuna Mac

Prep Time: 10 minutes   Cook Time: 15 minutes

2 cups water

2 cups (8 ounces) elbow macaroni, uncooked

¾ pound (12 ounces) VELVEETA Pasteurized Prepared Cheese
   Product, cut up

1 package (16 ounces) frozen vegetable blend, thawed, drained

1 can (6 ounces) tuna, drained, flaked

2 tablespoons milk

1. Bring water to boil in saucepan. Stir in macaroni. Reduce heat to medium-low; cover. Simmer 8 to 10 minutes or until macaroni is tender.

2. Add VELVEETA, vegetables, tuna and milk; stir until VELVEETA is melted.   *Makes 4 to 6 servings*

A Taste of Nutrition: With mixed vegetables, Tuna Mac is an excellent source of vitamin A. But you can also substitute any 16-ounce package of a frozen vegetable for the mixed vegetable blend if your family has a particular favorite.

Tuna Mac

QUICK FIXIN' DINNERS

These recipes are designed for quick and easy preparation. And to reflect that, we decided to name these recipes "Quick Fixin' Dinners." Notice how we dropped the "G" on the word "Fixing" to show how quickly these recipes can be made. By dropping the letter "G," we have created a visual cue, so the reader will be convinced that these really are quick recipes and that they should try them for that reason alone.

Ultimate Macaroni & Cheese

Prep Time: 5 minutes   Cook Time: 15 minutes

2 cups (8 ounces) elbow macaroni, uncooked

1 pound (16 ounces) VELVEETA Pasteurized Prepared Cheese Product, cut up

½ cup milk

Dash pepper

1. Cook macaroni as directed on package; drain well. Return to same pan.

2. Add VELVEETA, milk and pepper to same pan. Stir on low heat until VELVEETA is melted. Serve immediately.

Makes 4 to 6 servings

Ultimate Macaroni & Cheese

Barbecue Chicken Pizza

Prep Time: 15 minutes   **Bake Time:** 15 minutes

- 2 boneless skinless chicken breast halves (about ¾ pound), cut into thin strips
- 1 green pepper, cut into strips
- ¼ cup thinly sliced red onion
- 1 prepared pizza crust (12 inch)
- ⅓ cup BULL'S-EYE Original Barbecue Sauce
- 1 package (8 ounces) VELVEETA Mild Cheddar Shredded Pasteurized Process Cheese Food

1. Spray large skillet with no stick cooking spray. Add chicken, green pepper and onion; cook and stir on medium-high heat 4 to 5 minutes or until chicken is cooked through.

2. Place crust on cookie sheet. Spread with barbecue sauce. Top with chicken mixture and VELVEETA.

3. Bake at 375°F for 12 to 15 minutes or until VELVEETA is melted and crust is golden brown.   *Makes 4 to 6 servings*

Barbecue Chicken Pizza

15 Minute Cheesy Chili 'N Rice Skillet

1 pound ground beef

1 can (15 ounces) chili with beans

1 can (14½ ounces) diced tomatoes, undrained

1 cup water

2 cups MINUTE White Rice, uncooked

½ pound (8 ounces) VELVEETA Pasteurized Prepared Cheese
   Product, cut up

1. Brown meat in large skillet on medium-high heat; drain.

2. Add chili, tomatoes and water to skillet; stir. Bring to boil.

3. Stir in rice and VELVEETA; cover. Remove from heat. Let stand
5 minutes. Stir until VELVEETA is melted.   *Makes 4 servings*

Classic Potatoes Au Gratin

Prep Time: 25 minutes   Bake Time: 22 minutes

4 cups thinly sliced potatoes (about 4 to 5 medium)

½ pound (8 ounces) VELVEETA Pasteurized Prepared Cheese
    Product, cut up

½ cup chopped onion

1 teaspoon dry mustard

¼ teaspoon pepper

1. Cook potatoes in boiling water 18 minutes or until barely tender;
drain.

2. Toss potatoes and remaining ingredients in 2-quart casserole; cover.

3. Bake at 350°F for 20 to 22 minutes or until potatoes are tender. Stir
before serving.   *Makes 6 servings*

A Variation: Ham & Potatoes Au Gratin: For
an easy main dish, prepare as directed,
stirring in 1½ cups chopped ham with
remaining ingredients.

Creamy Chicken Broccoli Fettuccine

Prep Time: 10 minutes   Cook Time: 10 minutes

½ cup MIRACLE WHIP Salad Dressing

1 pound boneless skinless chicken breasts, cubed

1 package (10 ounces) frozen chopped broccoli, thawed

½ pound (8 ounces) VELVEETA Pasteurized Prepared Cheese Product, cut up

8 ounces fettuccine, cooked, drained

1. Heat salad dressing in large skillet. Add chicken; cook and stir on medium-high heat about 8 minutes or until cooked through.

2. Stir in broccoli and VELVEETA. Stir on low heat until VELVEETA is melted.

3. Add fettuccine. Toss until well coated.   *Makes 6 servings*

Take a Shortcut: *It's much easier to cut up chicken if it is still partially frozen. When using thawing chicken breast halves, cut the chicken into chunks while it is still partially frozen, then return to the refrigerator to allow to thaw completely.*

Creamy Chicken Broccoli Fettuccine

Cheesy Rice & Broccoli

Prep Time: 5 minutes   Cook Time: 10 minutes plus standing

1 package (10 ounces) frozen chopped broccoli, thawed, drained

1 cup water

1½ cups MINUTE White Rice, uncooked

½ pound (8 ounces) VELVEETA Pasteurized Prepared Cheese Product, cut up

1. Bring broccoli and water to full boil in medium saucepan on medium-high heat.

2. Stir in rice; cover. Remove from heat. Let stand 5 minutes.

3. Add VELVEETA; stir until VELVEETA is melted.   *Makes 6 servings*

Golden Sauce

Prep Time: 5 minutes   Cook Time: 10 minutes

½ pound (8 ounces) VELVEETA Pasteurized Prepared Cheese Product, cut up

¼ cup milk

1. Stir VELVEETA and milk in saucepan on low heat until smooth. Serve over hot cooked pasta or vegetables.   *Makes 1 cup*

<u>Microwave:</u> Microwave VELVEETA and milk in 1½-quart microwavable bowl on HIGH 2½ to 4½ minutes or until smooth, stirring every minute. Serve as directed.

Cheesy Rice & Broccoli

Cheesy Italian Chicken

Prep Time: 5 minutes   Cook Time: 20 minutes

4 boneless skinless chicken breast halves (about 1¼ pounds)

1 can (15 ounces) chunky Italian-style tomato sauce <u>or</u> 1 jar (15 ounces) chunky spaghetti sauce

½ pound (8 ounces) VELVEETA Pasteurized Prepared Cheese Product, cut up

Hot cooked pasta

1. Spray large skillet with no stick cooking spray. Add chicken; brown on medium-high heat 1 to 2 minutes on each side. Reduce heat to low.

2. Stir in tomato sauce; cover. Simmer 12 to 15 minutes or until chicken is cooked through.

3. Add VELVEETA; cover. Cook on low heat until VELVEETA is melted. Serve over pasta.   *Makes 4 servings*

Golden Mashed Potatoes

Prep Time: 30 minutes   Bake Time: 30 minutes

2½ cups cubed cooked potatoes, mashed

3 tablespoons milk

2 tablespoons butter <u>or</u> margarine

1 tablespoon chopped fresh chives

½ pound (8 ounces) VELVEETA Pasteurized Prepared Cheese
  Product, cut up, divided

¼ cup (1 ounce) KRAFT 100% Grated Parmesan Cheese

1. Beat potatoes, milk, butter and chives until fluffy. Stir in ½ of the
VELVEETA.

2. Spoon into 1-quart casserole; sprinkle with Parmesan cheese.

3. Bake at 350°F for 20 to 25 minutes or until thoroughly heated. Top
with remaining VELVEETA. Bake an additional 5 minutes or until
VELVEETA begins to melt.   *Makes 4 to 6 servings*

*<u>A Variation</u>: Garlic Mashed Potatoes: Prepare
as directed, adding ¾ teaspoon garlic
powder <u>or</u> 2 to 3 cloves garlic, minced, with
VELVEETA. Wait a few minutes before
increasing the amount of garlic you add,
as garlic flavor will build over time.*

Spicy Chicken Spaghetti

Prep Time: 5 minutes   Bake Time: 40 minutes

12 ounces spaghetti, uncooked

4 boneless skinless chicken breast halves (about 1¼ pounds),
    cut into strips

1 pound (16 ounces) VELVEETA Pasteurized Prepared Cheese
    Product, cut up

1 can (10¾ ounces) condensed cream of chicken soup

1 can (10 ounces) diced tomatoes and green chilies, undrained

1 can (4½ ounces) sliced mushrooms, drained

⅓ cup milk

1. Cook pasta as directed on package; drain. Return to same pan.

2. Spray skillet with no stick cooking spray. Add chicken; cook and stir
on medium-high heat 4 to 5 minutes or until cooked through. Add
VELVEETA, soup, tomatoes and green chilies, mushrooms and milk; stir
on low heat until VELVEETA is melted. Add chicken mixture to pasta;
toss to coat. Spoon into greased 13×9-inch baking dish.

3. Bake at 350°F for 35 to 40 minutes or until thoroughly heated.

Makes 6 to 8 servings

Spicy Chicken Spaghetti

15 Minute Cheesy Chicken & Vegetable Rice

1 tablespoon oil

4 small boneless skinless chicken breast halves
(about 1 pound)

1 can (14½ ounces) chicken broth <u>or</u> 1¾ cups water

2 cups MINUTE White Rice, uncooked

1 package (16 ounces) frozen vegetable blend (such as broccoli,
cauliflower and carrots), thawed, drained

¾ pound (12 ounces) VELVEETA Pasteurized Prepared Cheese
Product, cut up

1. Heat oil in large nonstick skillet on medium-high heat. Add chicken;
cover. Cook 4 minutes on each side or until cooked through. Remove
chicken from skillet.

2. Add broth to skillet. Bring to boil.

3. Stir in rice, vegetables and VELVEETA. Top with chicken; cover. Cook
on low heat 5 minutes. Stir until VELVEETA is melted.

Makes 4 servings

<u>Note:</u> Increase oil to 2 tablespoons if using regular skillet.

*15 Minute Cheesy Chicken &
Vegetable Rice*

Easy Pasta Primavera

Prep Time: 15 minutes   Cook Time: 20 minutes

3 cups (8 ounces) rotini, uncooked

2 cups water

1 package (16 ounces) frozen vegetable blend

¾ pound (12 ounces) VELVEETA LIGHT Pasteurized Prepared Cheese
    Product, cut up

2 tablespoons reduced fat milk

¼ teaspoon <u>each</u> garlic powder and pepper

1. Bring pasta and water to boil in saucepan; simmer 10 minutes or
until pasta is tender.

2. Add vegetables, VELVEETA LIGHT, milk and seasonings. Stir until
VELVEETA LIGHT is melted and mixture is thoroughly heated.

Makes 4 to 6 servings

Cheesy Rice

Prep Time: 5 minutes   Cook Time: 10 minutes plus standing

1½ cups water

2 cups MINUTE White Rice, uncooked

½ pound (8 ounces) VELVEETA Pasteurized Prepared Cheese
    Product, cut up

1. Bring water to boil in saucepan. Stir in rice and VELVEETA. Cook
and stir on low heat until VELVEETA is melted; cover. Remove from
heat. Let stand 5 minutes. Stir.   *Makes 4 (1-cup) servings*

Easy Pasta Primavera

Twice Baked Ranch Potatoes

Prep Time: 20 minutes plus baking potatoes   **Bake Time: 20 minutes**

- 4 baking potatoes
- ½ cup KRAFT Ranch Dressing
- ¼ cup BREAKSTONE'S <u>or</u> KNUDSEN Sour Cream
- 1 tablespoon OSCAR MAYER Real Bacon Bits
- ¼ pound (4 ounces) VELVEETA Pasteurized Prepared Cheese Product, cut up

1. Bake potatoes at 400°F for 1 hour. Slice off tops of potatoes; scoop out centers, leaving ⅛-inch shell.

2. Mash potatoes. Add dressing, sour cream and bacon bits; beat until fluffy. Stir VELVEETA into potato mixture. Spoon into shells.

3. Bake at 350°F for 20 minutes.   *Makes 4 servings*

<u>How to Bake Potatoes:</u> Russet potatoes are best for baking. Scrub potatoes well, blot dry and rub the skin with a little oil and salt. Prick the skin of the potatoes with a fork so steam can escape. Stand them on end in a muffin tin. Bake at 400°F for 60 minutes or until tender.

Twice Baked Ranch Potatoes

Cheesy Chicken & Rice Skillet

Prep Time: 5 minutes   Cook Time: 15 minutes

1 tablespoon oil

4 small boneless skinless chicken breast halves (about 1 pound)

1 can (10¾ ounces) condensed cream of chicken soup

1 soup can (1⅓ cups) water

2 cups MINUTE White Rice, uncooked

1 package (8 ounces) VELVEETA Shredded Pasteurized Process
   Cheese Food, divided

1. Heat oil in large nonstick skillet on medium-high heat. Add chicken; cover. Cook 4 minutes on each side or until cooked through. Remove chicken from skillet.

2. Add soup and water to skillet; stir. Bring to boil.

3. Stir in rice and 1 cup of the VELVEETA. Top with chicken. Sprinkle with remaining VELVEETA; cover. Cook on low heat 5 minutes.

Makes 4 servings

<u>Note:</u> Increase oil to 2 tablespoons if using regular skillet.

<u>How to Cook Chicken:</u> A general rule for chicken doneness is when the juices run clear and the meat is no longer pink. If you use a thermometer, the internal temperature in the thickest part of the chicken breast should reach 170°F.

Cheesy Chicken & Rice Skillet

MEXICAN MADNESS

Your self-control slowly diminishes, your eyes widen and your taste buds begin to pulsate...you have been diagnosed with Mexican Madness. This condition may sound a little scary and intimidating, but once you expose yourself and others to these recipes you will discover that being absolutely mad is a blessing and should be cherished and spread to others.

Tex-Mex Chicken & Rice

Prep Time: 5 minutes   Cook Time: 15 minutes

4 small boneless skinless chicken breast halves (about 1 pound)

1 can (15 ounces) pinto beans, drained or 1½ cups cooked pinto beans

1 can (14½ ounces) chicken broth

1 cup TACO BELL HOME ORIGINALS Thick 'N Chunky Salsa

2 cups MINUTE White Rice, uncooked

½ pound (8 ounces) VELVEETA Pasteurized Prepared Cheese Product, cut up

1. Spray large skillet with no stick cooking spray. Add chicken; cover. Cook on medium-high heat 4 minutes on each side or until cooked through. Remove chicken from skillet.

2. Add beans, broth and salsa to skillet; stir. Bring to boil.

3. Stir in rice and VELVEETA. Top with chicken; cover. Cook on low heat 5 minutes. Sprinkle with chopped cilantro, if desired, before serving.

Makes 4 servings

Tex-Mex Chicken & Rice

Speedy Spicy Quesadillas

Prep Time: 5 minutes   Microwave Time: 3 minutes

½ pound (8 ounces) VELVEETA Mexican Pasteurized Process Cheese Spread with Jalapeño Peppers, cut into 8 slices

8 flour tortillas (6 inch)

1. Place 1 VELVEETA slice on each tortilla. Fold tortillas in half. Place 2 tortillas on microwavable plate.

2. Microwave on HIGH 30 to 45 seconds or until VELVEETA is melted. Repeat with remaining tortillas. Cut each tortilla in half. Serve with BREAKSTONE'S or KNUDSEN Sour Cream, tomato and guacamole, if desired.   *Makes 16 servings*

Easy Additions: Try adding 1 slice of OSCAR MAYER Ham for a more filling sandwich. Or top VELVEETA on each quesadilla with 1 tablespoon OSCAR MAYER Real Bacon Bits.

Speedy Spicy Quesadillas

Cheesy Tacos

Prep Time: 5 minutes   Cook Time: 15 minutes

1 pound ground beef

¼ cup water

1 package (1¼ ounces) TACO BELL HOME ORIGINALS Taco
    Seasoning Mix

¾ pound (12 ounces) VELVEETA Mexican Pasteurized Process
    Cheese Spread with Jalapeño Peppers, cut up

1 package (4.5 ounces) TACO BELL HOME ORIGINALS Taco Shells
    or 12 flour tortillas (8 inch)

1. Brown meat in large skillet; drain. Stir in water and taco seasoning
mix.

2. Add VELVEETA; stir on low heat until VELVEETA is melted.

3. Fill heated taco shells with meat mixture. Top with your favorite
toppings, such as shredded lettuce, chopped tomato and TACO BELL
HOME ORIGINALS Thick 'N Chunky Salsa.   *Makes 4 to 6 servings*

 *Serving Suggestion: Cheesy Tacos are a fun family dinner. Have your child place the family's favorite taco toppings, such as shredded lettuce and chopped tomato, in a muffin tin to pass around at the table.*

Cheesy Tacos

Beef Enchiladas Olé

Prep Time: 20 minutes   Microwave Time: 6 minutes

- 1 pound ground beef <u>or</u> 1 pound boneless skinless chicken breasts, chopped
- 1 cup TACO BELL HOME ORIGINALS Thick 'N Chunky Salsa, divided
- 1 pound (16 ounces) VELVEETA Mexican Pasteurized Process Cheese Spread with Jalapeño Peppers, cut up, divided
- 10 flour tortillas

1. Brown meat; drain. Stir in ½ cup of the salsa and ½ of the VELVEETA; cook and stir on medium-low heat until VELVEETA is melted.

2. Spoon ¼ cup meat mixture in center of each tortilla; roll up. Place tortillas, seam-side down, in microwavable baking dish. Top with remaining ½ cup salsa and VELVEETA. Cover loosely with microwavable plastic wrap.

3. Microwave on HIGH 4 to 6 minutes or until VELVEETA is melted.

Makes 5 servings

<u>Choosing Flour Tortillas</u>: Flour tortillas come in many colors and sizes. You'll find them in the refrigerated dairy case or grocery aisle of the supermarket. You'll also find tortillas in a variety of flavors such as herbs, tomato or spinach which are fine to substitute in Beef Enchiladas Olé.

Beef Enchiladas Olé

Taco Chicken

PrepTime: 10 minutes   Cook Time: 15 minutes

4 boneless skinless chicken breast halves (about 1¼ pounds), cut into chunks

2¼ cups water

1½ cups MINUTE White Rice, uncooked

1 package (1¼ ounces) TACO BELL HOME ORIGINALS Taco Seasoning Mix

¾ pound (12 ounces) VELVEETA Mexican Pasteurized Process Cheese Spread with Jalapeño Peppers, cut up

1 package (10 ounces) frozen corn, thawed

½ cup canned black beans, rinsed, drained

1. Spray large skillet with no stick cooking spray. Add chicken; cook and stir on medium-high heat 2 minutes or until no longer pink.

2. Stir in water, rice and seasoning mix. Bring to boil. Reduce heat to medium-low; cover. Simmer 8 to 10 minutes or until water is absorbed.

3. Add VELVEETA, corn and beans; stir until VELVEETA is melted.

Makes 6 servings

Cheesy Mexican Chicken Skillet

Prep Time: 5 minutes   Cook Time: 20 minutes plus standing

4 small boneless skinless chicken breast halves (about 1 pound)

1½ cups water

1 can (10¾ ounces) condensed cream of chicken soup

1 package (1¼ ounces) TACO BELL HOME ORIGINALS Taco Seasoning Mix

2 cups MINUTE White Rice, uncooked

1 package (8 ounces) VELVEETA Mexican Shredded Pasteurized Process Cheese Food, divided

1. Spray large nonstick skillet with no stick cooking spray. Add chicken; cover. Cook on medium-high heat 4 minutes on each side or until cooked through. Remove chicken from skillet.

2. Add water, soup and seasoning mix to skillet; bring to boil. Stir in rice and 1 cup of the VELVEETA. Top with chicken. Reduce heat to low; cover. Cook 5 minutes.

3. Sprinkle with remaining 1 cup VELVEETA; cover. Let stand 1 to 2 minutes or until VELVEETA is melted.   *Makes 4 servings*

Jalapeño Pepper Steak

Prep Time: 15 minutes   Cook Time: 10 minutes

1 pound sirloin steak <u>or</u> boneless chicken, cut into strips

1 package (16 ounces) frozen bell pepper and onion strips,
    thawed, drained <u>or</u> 3 cups fresh bell pepper and onion strips

¾ pound (12 ounces) VELVEETA Mexican Pasteurized Process
    Cheese Spread with Jalapeño Peppers, cut up

1. Spray large skillet with no stick cooking spray. Add steak; cook on
high heat 2 minutes or until no longer pink; remove from skillet.

2. Stir in vegetables; cook 2 minutes. Reduce heat to medium-low.

3. Add VELVEETA; stir until melted. Stir in steak. Serve over hot cooked
MINUTE White Rice or on tortillas.   *Makes 6 servings*

10 Minute Cheesy Mexican Rice

1 can (10½ ounces) condensed chicken broth (1⅓ cups)

1 cup TACO BELL HOME ORIGINALS Thick 'N Chunky Salsa

2 cups MINUTE White Rice, uncooked

¼ pound (4 ounces) VELVEETA Pasteurized Prepared Cheese
    Product, cut up

1. Bring broth and salsa to boil in medium saucepan.

2. Stir in rice and VELVEETA; cover. Remove from heat. Let stand
5 minutes. Stir until VELVEETA is melted.   *Makes 6 servings*

Jalapeño Pepper Steak

Grilled Chicken Fajitas

Prep Time: 10 minutes   Grill Time: 20 minutes

3 boneless skinless chicken breast halves (about ¾ pound)

1 clove garlic, halved

1 medium green <u>or</u> red pepper, quartered

½ red onion, sliced ¼-inch thick

1½ cups VELVEETA Shredded Pasteurized Process Cheese Food

6 flour tortillas (6 inch), warmed

TACO BELL HOME ORIGINALS Thick 'N Chunky Salsa

1. Rub both sides of chicken with garlic. Place chicken, green pepper and onion slices on greased grill over medium-hot coals.

2. Grill 20 minutes or until cooked through, turning occasionally. Cut chicken and green pepper into thin strips.

3. Spoon chicken mixture and ¼ cup VELVEETA in center of each tortilla; fold. Serve with salsa.   *Makes 6 servings*

<u>Use Your Stove</u>: Cut chicken into strips. Spray skillet with no stick cooking spray. Add chicken and 1 clove garlic, minced; cook and stir on medium-high heat 5 minutes. Add green pepper, cut into strips, and onion; cook and stir 4 to 5 minutes or until chicken is cooked through and vegetables are tender-crisp. Continue as directed.

Grilled Chicken Fajitas

Chicken Enchilada Casserole

Prep Time: 15 minutes   Bake Time: 35 minutes

2 cups chopped cooked chicken

1 can (10¾ ounces) condensed cream of chicken soup

½ pound (8 ounces) VELVEETA Mexican Pasteurized Process Cheese
   Spread with Jalapeño Peppers, cut up

8 corn tortillas (6 inch)

½ cup TACO BELL HOME ORIGINALS Thick 'N Chunky Salsa

1. Mix chicken, soup and VELVEETA.

2. Spread 1 cup of the chicken mixture on bottom of 12×8-inch baking dish; cover with 4 of the tortillas. Top with ¼ cup of the salsa and 1 cup of the remaining chicken mixture. Repeat layers with 4 tortillas, remaining ¼ cup salsa and remaining chicken mixture.

3. Bake, uncovered, at 350°F for 30 to 35 minutes or until thoroughly heated. Top with additional salsa, if desired.   *Makes 6 servings*

<u>Great Substitutes</u>: *Don't have leftover chicken? Just look in the refrigerated meat case of your supermarket for prepared cooked chicken such as LOUIS RICH CARVING BOARD Chicken Breast Strips.*

Cheesy Salsa Chicken & Rice

Prep Time: 10 minutes   Cook Time: 10 minutes plus standing

4 boneless skinless chicken breast halves (about 1¼ pound), cut
into chunks

1 cup TACO BELL HOME ORIGINALS Thick 'N Chunky Salsa

½ cup water

½ pound (8 ounces) VELVEETA Pasteurized Prepared Cheese
Product, cut up

1½ cups MINUTE White Rice, uncooked

1. Spray large skillet with no stick cooking spray. Add chicken; cook
and stir on medium-high heat 4 to 5 minutes or until cooked through.

2. Add salsa, water and VELVEETA to skillet. Bring to boil.

3. Stir in rice; cover. Remove from heat. Let stand 7 minutes or until
liquid is absorbed and rice is tender. Stir before serving.

Makes 4 servings

SUPER DUPER SOUPS AND SANDWICHES

Since achieving the title, "Super Duper," our soups and sandwiches have not been acting quite the same way as they once did. Unfortunately, the title of "Super Duper" has gone to their heads. They have alienated all other soups and sandwiches, refusing to associate themselves with lesser forms of nourishment. We do, however, feel somewhat responsible since we were the ones who made these recipes so good.

Ultimate Grilled Cheese

Prep Time: 5 minutes   Cook Time: 10 minutes

2 slices bread

2 ounces VELVEETA Pasteurized Prepared Cheese Product, sliced

2 teaspoons soft margarine

1. Top 1 bread slice with VELVEETA and second bread slice.

2. Spread outside of sandwich with margarine.

3. Cook in skillet on medium heat until lightly browned on both sides.

Makes 1 sandwich

Ultimate Grilled Cheese

Cheesy Chicken Ranch Sandwiches

Prep Time: 5 minutes   Broil Time: 14 minutes

6 boneless skinless chicken breast halves (about 2 pounds)

⅔ cup KRAFT Ranch Dressing, divided

½ pound (8 ounces) VELVEETA Pasteurized Prepared Cheese Product, sliced

6 French bread rolls, split

Lettuce

1. Brush chicken with ⅓ cup of the dressing. Spray rack of broiler pan with no stick cooking spray. Place chicken on rack of broiler pan.

2. Broil 3 to 4 inches from heat 5 to 6 minutes on each side or until cooked through. Top chicken with VELVEETA. Broil an additional 2 minutes or until VELVEETA is melted.

3. Spread rolls with remaining dressing; fill with lettuce and chicken.

Makes 6 sandwiches

Use Your Grill: Prepare chicken as directed. Grill over hot coals 5 to 6 minutes on each side or until cooked through. Top with VELVEETA and continue grilling until VELVEETA is melted. Continue as directed.

Cheesy Chicken Ranch Sandwich

Cheesy Spinach Soup

Prep Time: 5 minutes   Cook Time: 10 minutes

¼ cup chopped onion

1 tablespoon reduced calorie margarine

2 cups skim milk

¾ pound (12 ounces) VELVEETA LIGHT Pasteurized Prepared Cheese Product, cut up

1 package (10 ounces) frozen chopped spinach, cooked, well drained

⅛ teaspoon ground nutmeg

Dash pepper

1. Cook and stir onion in reduced calorie margarine in 2-quart saucepan until tender.

2. Add remaining ingredients; stir on low heat until VELVEETA LIGHT is melted and mixture is thoroughly heated.

Makes 4 (1-cup) servings

Use Your Microwave: *Microwave onion and reduced calorie margarine in 2-quart microwavable casserole on HIGH 30 seconds to 1 minute or until onion is tender. Stir in remaining ingredients. Microwave 6 to 8 minutes or until thoroughly heated, stirring every 3 minutes.*

Chunky Chicken & Rice Soup

4 boneless skinless chicken breast halves (about 1¼ pounds), cubed

2 cups sliced mushrooms

½ cup chopped onion

½ cup coarsely chopped carrot

2 cups water

1 can (14½ ounces) chicken broth

1 cup MINUTE White Rice, uncooked

½ pound (8 ounces) VELVEETA Pasteurized Prepared Cheese Product, cut up

Salt and pepper

1. Spray large saucepan with no stick cooking spray. Add chicken; cook and stir on medium-high heat 2 to 3 minutes. Add vegetables. Cook 5 to 7 minutes or until chicken is thoroughly cooked and vegetables are tender, stirring occasionally.

2. Stir in water, broth and rice. Bring to boil; simmer 10 minutes.

3. Add VELVEETA; stir on low heat until VELVEETA is melted. Season to taste with salt and pepper.   *Makes 7 cups*

Beef Barley Soup

½ pound ground beef

2½ cups water

1 can (14½ ounces) stewed tomatoes, cut up

3 medium carrots, sliced

¾ cup sliced mushrooms

½ cup quick barley, uncooked

2 cloves garlic, minced

1 teaspoon dried oregano leaves, crushed

½ pound (8 ounces) VELVEETA Pasteurized Prepared Cheese Product, cut up

Salt and pepper

1. Brown meat in large saucepan; drain. Stir in water, tomatoes, carrots, mushrooms, barley, garlic and oregano.

2. Bring to boil. Reduce heat to low; cover. Simmer 10 minutes or until barley is tender.

3. Add VELVEETA; stir until melted. Season to taste with salt and pepper.

Makes 6 (1-cup) servings

Beef Barley Soup

BBQ Bacon Cheeseburgers

Prep Time: 10 minutes   Broil Time: 12 minutes

1 pound ground beef

2 tablespoons KRAFT Original Barbecue Sauce

¼ pound (4 ounces) VELVEETA Pasteurized Prepared Cheese Product, sliced

4 hamburger rolls, split, toasted

Lettuce

8 slices OSCAR MAYER Bacon, crisply cooked

1. Mix meat and barbecue sauce. Shape into 4 patties.

2. Broil patties 4 to 6 inches from heat or grill over hot coals 4 to 6 minutes on each side or to desired doneness, turning and brushing occasionally with additional barbecue sauce. Top each patty with VELVEETA. Continue broiling or grilling until VELVEETA begins to melt.

3. Fill rolls with cheeseburgers, lettuce and bacon.

Makes 4 sandwiches

Choosing Ground Beef: Ground sirloin will make the leanest hamburgers, then ground round, ground chuck and then ground beef. But remember, the leaner the ground beef, the drier the meat will be.

BBQ Bacon Cheeseburgers

Cheesy Beer Soup

Prep Time: 5 minutes   Cook Time: 10 minutes

½ cup chopped onion

1 tablespoon butter <u>or</u> margarine

1 pound (16 ounces) VELVEETA Pasteurized Prepared Cheese
   Product, cut up

1 can (10¾ ounces) condensed chicken broth, undiluted

½ cup beer

¼ teaspoon <u>each</u> white pepper and Worcestershire sauce

2 tablespoons OSCAR MAYER Real Bacon Bits

1. Cook and stir onion in butter in large saucepan on medium-high heat until tender.

2. Add VELVEETA, broth, beer, pepper and Worcestershire sauce. Stir constantly on low heat 5 minutes or until VELVEETA is melted and soup is hot.

3. Pour into 4 serving bowls; sprinkle with bacon bits.

Makes 4 (1-cup) servings

Cheeseburger Joe

Prep Time: 10 minutes   Cook Time: 15 minutes

1 pound ground beef

½ pound (12 ounces) VELVEETA Pasteurized Prepared Cheese
    Product, cut up

¼ cup catsup

1 to 2 teaspoons onion powder

1 teaspoon KRAFT Pure Prepared Mustard (optional)

6 hamburger buns, split

1. Brown meat in skillet; drain.

2. Add VELVEETA, catsup, onion powder and mustard; reduce heat to
medium-low. Stir until VELVEETA is melted. Serve in buns.

Makes 6 servings

*Serving Suggestion: To make these
sandwiches less messy, buy unsliced
hamburger buns and cut off the top quarter
of each bun. Hollow out the bottom part of
the bun, then spoon Cheeseburger Joe into
the bun and replace the top.*

Cheesy Broccoli Soup

Prep Time: 10 minutes   Cook Time: 15 minutes

¼ cup chopped onion

1 tablespoon butter <u>or</u> margarine

1½ cups milk

¾ pound (12 ounces) VELVEETA Pasteurized Prepared Cheese Product, cut up

1 package (10 ounces) frozen chopped broccoli, thawed, drained

Dash pepper

1. Cook and stir onion in butter in large saucepan on medium-high heat until tender.

2. Add remaining ingredients; stir on low heat until VELVEETA is melted and soup is thoroughly heated.   *Makes 4 (¾-cup) servings*

<u>Use Your Microwave</u>: Microwave onion and butter in 2-quart microwaveable casserole or bowl on HIGH 30 seconds to 1 minute or until onion is tender. Add remaining ingredients; mix well. Microwave 6 to 8 minutes or until VELVEETA is melted and soup is thoroughly heated, stirring every 3 minutes.

Cheesy Broccoli Soup

Hearty Chili

Prep Time: 15 minutes   Cook Time: 30 minutes

1 pound ground beef

¾ cup chopped onion

2 cans (14½ ounces each) tomatoes, coarsely chopped

1 can (16 ounces) kidney beans, drained

1 cup water

1 tablespoon chili powder

¼ teaspoon salt

1 package (8 ounces) VELVEETA Shredded Pasteurized Process Cheese Food

1. Brown meat in skillet; drain. Add onion; cook and stir until tender.

2. Stir in tomatoes, beans, water and seasonings; simmer 25 minutes, stirring occasionally.

3. Sprinkle with VELVEETA.   *Makes about 6 cups*

Hearty Chili

Tuna Sandwich Melts

Prep Time: 15 minutes   Bake Time: 25 minutes

1 can (6 ounces) tuna in water, drained, flaked

½ cup MIRACLE WHIP Salad Dressing

¼ pound (4 ounces) VELVEETA Pasteurized Prepared Cheese
  Product, cut up

½ cup sliced celery

¼ cup chopped onion

4 Kaiser rolls, split

1. Mix all ingredients except rolls.

2. Fill each roll with ⅓ cup tuna mixture; wrap in foil.

3. Bake at 375°F for 20 to 25 minutes or until thoroughly heated.

Makes 4 sandwiches

Use Your Microwave: Prepare sandwiches as directed except for wrapping in foil. Place 2 sandwiches on paper towel. Microwave on HIGH 1 minute or until thoroughly heated. Repeat with remaining sandwiches.

Cheesy Baked Potato Soup

Prep Time: 15 minutes plus baking potatoes   **Cook Time:** 15 minutes

¾ cup chopped onion

2 tablespoons butter <u>or</u> margarine

2 cups water

1 can (14½ ounces) chicken broth

2 to 3 large baked potatoes, cubed

Dash pepper

¾ pound (12 ounces) VELVEETA Pasteurized Prepared Cheese
Product, cut up

1. Cook and stir onion in butter in large saucepan on medium-high heat until tender.

2. Stir in water, broth, potatoes and pepper; heat thoroughly.

3. Add VELVEETA; stir on low heat until melted. Serve with bacon bits, BREAKSTONE'S or KNUDSEN Sour Cream and chopped fresh parsley, if desired. *Makes 6 cups*

Spicy Southwest Corn Cheese Soup

Prep Time: 15 minutes   Cook Time: 10 minutes

1 package (10 ounces) frozen sweet corn, thawed, drained

1 clove garlic, minced

1 tablespoon butter <u>or</u> margarine

¾ pound (12 ounces) VELVEETA Pasteurized Prepared Cheese Product, cut up

1 can (4 ounces) chopped green chilies

¾ cup chicken broth

¾ cup milk

2 tablespoons chopped fresh cilantro

1. Cook and stir corn and garlic in butter in large saucepan on medium-high heat until tender. Reduce heat to medium.

2. Stir in remaining ingredients; cook until VELVEETA is melted and soup is thoroughly heated. Top each serving with crushed tortilla chips, if desired.   *Makes 4 (1-cup) servings*

A Taste of Nutrition: A serving of Spicy Southwest Corn Cheese Soup is high in calcium. In addition, it is also an excellent source of vitamins A and C.

INDEX